Viking LinkedIn Marketing Page

Viking LinkedIn Marketing Page

Chapter 1:
Introduction

LinkedIn isn't just for helping you recruit top talent or finding your dream job, but is a powerful means of organic B2B marketing. You can of course leverage paid marketing on LinkedIn, but even with paid marketing every business needs to invest in building their organic presence. Just as with other social media platforms, LinkedIn is a global site—which is an effective means of growing your business well beyond your local service area. While B2B marketing is the most effective, don't discount LinkedIn for B2C.

The Numbers Are Impressive

LinkedIn is a site dedicated to professional so the mindset when joining, posting, searching, and networking is quite unique when compared to Facebook or Twitter. While the site may not be as saturated, that is something you can use to your advantage. Users join and log in for professional purposes, meaning you have a built-in captive audience. Just take a look at some of the stats:

- There are over 467 million users in over 200 countries around the world.
- The US has the largest number of users, followed by India, Brazil, Great Britain, and Canada.
- LinkedIn is available in over 24 languages.
- There are 1.5 million professional LinkedIn Groups in hundreds of industries.
- 57% of users are male and 44% are female.
- 41% of millionaires use LinkedIn.
- 13% of users are between the ages of 15 and 34—including over 40 million students and recent college grads.

- 94% of online marketers use LinkedIn to distribute content.
- 71% of professionals believe LinkedIn is a credible source for professional content.
- 80% of B2B leads come from LinkedIn.
- 46% of B2B social media traffic comes from LinkedIn.

So obviously, LinkedIn is the perfect place to market your business. Next, we'll talk about establishing marketing goals.

Chapter 2:

LinkedIn

Marketing

Goals

Establishing marketing goals is critical to the success of your LinkedIn marketing. Countless entrepreneurs and businesses have setup an LinkedIn presence, made a few posts, and then let it sit untouched for months or even years. This is usually due to a lack or absence of goals. So, before you even begin establishing any sort of LinkedIn presence or strategy, you need to establish clear marketing goals.

Your goals should be specific, measurable, and attainable. They can be long term, short term, or a mix of both. Deadlines and milestones can be helpful as well. "I want to increase my social following" would be an example of a bad goal that will likely result in your marketing efforts petering out after a while because there are no specific milestones. "I want to gain 1,000 likes by Christmas" is an example of a good goal. It's specific, measurable, and certainly attainable. Below are some examples of the various goal categories you might be interested in.

Traffic to Website (Sales, Leads, Content)

Probably one of the most popular goals of LinkedIn Marketing is to funnel your LinkedIn traffic back to your own web properties. After all, most businesses don't do business "on" LinkedIn. You're leveraging LinkedIn to obtain traffic and convert that LinkedIn traffic into brand-followers, leads, prospects, and customers. So maybe your goal is to get people to a landing page with a free offer where they can subscribe to your list and become a lead. Maybe they're being sent to a sales page or an eCommerce store. Maybe you just want to do some content marketing and send them to your blog. Whatever the case, the end goal for a lot of businesses will likely be bringing LinkedIn traffic AWAY from LinkedIn and over to their own web properties.

Social Following (aka LinkedIn as Autoresponder)

In this goal category, your aim is to build a large number of followers. The reason we also refer to this as "LinkedIn as Autoresponder" is because the main sought-after benefit here is to increase the number of people who will see your posts in their feeds. In this sense, your LinkedIn posts become similar to sending out email broadcasts via your autoresponder. If you grow a large enough community, this can be very beneficial and if your content is engaging enough to get a lot of traction in the form of likes, comments, and shares, you can significantly increase the range of your organic reach into people's feeds.

Passive Presence

Some businesses might have purely passive goals. Simply being present and discoverable inside LinkedIn is a benefit that has wider appeal and greater utility than you may think. In many cases, a company's LinkedIn presence might supersede or at least augment what was once the role of a website or blog. When people come across this content of yours and look at your account they can see some basic info about your brand or business and you can get some traffic to your website. This same approach can also be used for events, communities, and brands.

Brand Awareness

Another goal that's less thought about might be spreading brand awareness and recognition. If you're just starting out, there's a good chance your brand might be in need of a jumpstart. If nobody's ever heard of you, a great way to increase recognition is to simply create and share unique, helpful, or entertaining content and get your name, logo, and overall brand identity in front of as many people as possible as many times as possible. If this is your goal, you want to avoid being salesy in the beginning. Ensure you're focused almost entirely on posting helpful, relevant, or entertaining content.

Expand Existing Audiences

If you've already got an audience, your goal might be to make it bigger. This can be done via several social marketing methods. Sharing viral content, either curated or created yourself, can lead to a huge increase in your LinkedIn audience. Although creating your own viral content like that can be great, if you don't have the time or means to do so, you can simply leverage existing content that's already proven itself to be viral by curating/re-sharing it with your own comments or angle added to it. Also, a few humorous images and memes can't hurt either, but keep in mind LinkedIn is a little more professional than other platforms, so don't go overboard with the humor. Other ways to expand existing audiences can include contests, sweepstakes, and gamification. Assuming your offers/prizes are compelling enough, incentivized sharing/following can be very effective. Just ensure your methods are permitted by LinkedIn's Terms of Service.

Enhancing or Repairing Public Relations

Do you want to set your company apart in the public eye? Do you want to associate your brand with feelings of good will and community involvement? Was your business recently involved in a controversial incident that requires damage control?

It doesn't take a humiliating public catastrophe to make PR enhancement a good idea. This is a goal that any business can engage in. Non-sales related campaigns can include photos or videos that foster positive values and goodwill or even involvement in social movements (be careful not alienate half your prospects) and noble causes. Did your business recently donate to a charity, build a school in a third world country, serve food at a local pantry? These are all things to post about. These don't necessarily need to be about things that your business participated in. They can be content about general things like a heart-warming video about helping the poor or caring for the elderly. Special holidays like Christmas, Thanksgiving, or Mother's Day also present opportunities to leverage emotions, foster goodwill, and enhance your PR.

Market Research

A hugely beneficial goal of LinkedIn marketing is market research. If you're just starting your business or going down a new path, LinkedIn can be an excellent place to learn more about your audience and your market. This can be done in a structured way with things like surveys and questionnaires, or in a less structured way by simply engaging with your audience, commenting, asking questions, and so on. Also, lurking or conversing in LinkedIn areas or content related to your industry can teach you a ton about what your customers want and who they are. Beyond that, you can monitor your competitors' accounts, groups, and posts to see what their customers like and what they're complaining about so you can adjust your business accordingly. Creating your own group, posting, and engaging within it is another great way to get a constant stream of market/audience data flowing into your business. Ultimately, your goal should be to come up with one or two ideal customer avatars that you can then base your marketing and product development on.

All of the goals you've learned about in this section require some sort of presence on LinkedIn. Getting that presence started is what we're going to talk about next.

Chapter 3:

Getting

Started   On

LinkedIn

The first step in getting started on LinkedIn is setting up your Company Page. This is the place that people will be directed if they type your business name into your website. The concept of a Company Page is a bit similar to a Facebook newsfeed, but allows you to post static content that can be updated at any time. This includes:

- Your company logo
- Your industry
- A unique "About Us" section
- A company section with details such as: website URL, Headquarters, Company Type, Company Size, and area of Specialty

Your Company Page is a public page, where anyone who would like to can follow you, view your current job openings, or click on a list of your current employees. Update your Company Page at least once each quarter. As an added bonus, each time it is updated it will send an update notification to all of your followers—which is an excellent way to keep you top of mind. The same type of notification is sent when you update your personal profile.

Below the static information above is your Recent Updates which we will discuss in detail a bit later.

Your First Followers Should Be Your Employees

Now that your Company Page is set up, it's time to send out an email to your current employees. Request that they both follow you, and update their personal LinkedIn profiles to ensure they select you as their current employer. Since leads can click directly to your current employees from your Company Page, it is also a good time to request that your entire team—but especially your key players, update their LinkedIn profiles with their most recent accomplishments.

Generating Skill Confirmations And Endorsements

Now is also an excellent time to hop on and start confirming your employee's skillsets, and writing endorsements. This is a strategy that has a two-fold positive ripple effect. First, it encourages your employees to reciprocate. Second, there is nothing that speaks more than team members who enthusiastically endorse their colleagues.

Utilizing Your Contact Lists To Expand Your 1st Degree Connections

Your 1st Degree connections are LinkedIn members who you are directly following; personally, not their Company Pages. Take the time every 4 to 6 months to sync your professional email contact lists with LinkedIn to ensure you are connected with your most recent contacts and colleagues. Also, utilize the built-in automated suggestion tools to find more connections. This is also an excellent method of keeping your business top of mind when you have only had a brief meeting or introduction with a potential lead—such as at a conference or networking event.

Just as with your employee skills and endorsements, endorse your contacts and connections. However, don't just give away random skills and endorsements with the intention of getting more in return. Instead, give sincere feedback that you would be proud to back up in person. Also, avoid the temptation to randomly connect with 2nd and 3rd degree contacts unless you are genuinely looking to network.

Chapter 4:

LinkedIn

Pages &

Groups

Now that you have a Company Page and a steadily growing list of connections, it is time to start driving traffic and engagement. Your initial goal is to increase your number of followers, then accelerating your likes and comments.

Add LinkedIn Buttons to Your Website and A Link Where Needed

The first thing you want to do is to add a LinkedIn (and other social media) button to your website. One button should be added to your Home page and to the static header or footer. This button will direct users right to your Company Page where they will hopefully follow you and engage.

Next up, you want to add social media share options to your blog posts. This will either allow leads who read your blog to automatically share the post to their LinkedIn or social media feeds, or to "like" or comment on your post.

Last but not least, always be on the lookout for appropriate places to add your LinkedIn URL. This includes both your Company Page and your personal URL. This includes your email, relevant online marketing, and internal links on your articles and blog posts.

Posting Relevant Content on Your Company Page

When it comes to sharing content on your Company Page you must be strategic. The items you post will show up in the Recent Updates section of your Company Page. The goal is not to post for the sake of posting, but to post content that would be meaningful and valuable to your industry and your followers. This includes original content, as well as content that you share from other sources. Aim for no more than one post a day, 3 to 7 days a week. To save time, preschedule your posts using a tool such as Hootsuite or Buffer. You can even link Buffer to a content suggestion tool such as Quuu. Consider posting varied content to each social platform, and yes you can post content that does well more than once—just spread it out so that it posts at least one week later.

Make sure that everything you post has a relevant headline, or asks an engaging question. Here are a few ideas of content that can drive likes, engagement, and followers:

Share Relevant Articles from Others—if you find a trending, recent, or otherwise relevant article on another online platform, feel free to share it on your page. This includes articles from online newspapers, magazines, industry blogs, videos, or any URL.

Your Blog Posts—if you post blogs, articles, news, or company updates to your website you should always share them on your Company Page. This includes old posts on topics that are trending at the moment.

Links to Upcoming Events—an upcoming company charity fundraiser or special event or the upcoming industry workshop or seminar you will be attending, go ahead and add it to your page.

Infographics—infographics are an excellent method of driving engagement, and great infographics are something people like to share. The infographic will need to be shared from another ULR.

Original Content Curated Just for LinkedIn—You cannot publish content straight to your Company Page, but you can have content curated to post to your (or one of your key players) personal profiles. Once posted, you can share the URL to this post on your Company Page.

Something Fun or Informative—Also explore links to relevant cartoons, fun trending topics or something informative such as a great eBook that you just read, or a webinar you recently attended.

Create a SlideShare—create new SlideShare or add existing SlideShare to your profile. These will automatically populate in the Summary section of your personal profile, to then be shared on your Company Page. You can also invest in SlideShare content ads.

You Don't Have to Curate Your Own Content

To save time and stress, don't feel obligated to create any of the content suggestions above. Your inhouse marketing team or graphic designer can create your content, or you can outsource your content to a ghostwriter or freelancer.

Leveraging LinkedIn Groups

Now that you have a nice solid foundation, it's time to start expanding your personal following—and leveraging relevant LinkedIn Groups is an excellent way to do just that. The groups you join should be strategic; a nice mix of industry groups and groups your target B2B audience is likely to frequent. However, also consider creating your own LinkedIn Groups. At current moment, you can be a member of up to 100 groups of the current 1.5 million groups, and can own or manage up to 30. Below we will discuss the advantages of both—but keep in mind that more is not always better.

Establishing Yourself as a Thought Leader Is Your Number 1 Goal

Your goal may be to generate more leads via organic marketing, and there is no better way to achieve this than to establish yourself as an industry innovator or thought leader. This means that the articles you share in groups, the posts you write, polls you create, questions you ask, and the comments you make should be far more thought provoking than the often casual comments and posts shared within your personal Facebook or Twitter profiles. In other words, don't comment just to comment—or just to agree with others, but with the intention of adding value.

Joining New Groups

Odds are you only have time to regularly engage in a handful of groups, so 10 or less is more than fine. You won't be able to see how active the group is until you request to join and are approved, but you are looking for active groups—or new and fast-growing groups. When scrolling through the group database consider factors such as:

- Number of members in the group.
- What company/companies the group admins work for.
- The service area the bulk of the members are in, and if it's a service area you serve.
- Membership criteria and rules.

Once approved, set a goal for how many days a week you want to engage. However, you must make responding to comments and direct messaging a priority—above and beyond your new posts and engagement. Keep in mind, that trying to sell your product or service is not the goal. In fact, doing either will likely get you removed from the group.

As you identify other members, potential leads, or industry influencers, connect with them directly—then message them directly. Better yet, when someone is impressed with your contributions and though leadership—they will connect with you directly or visit your Company Page.

Creating Your Own Group

Creating your own group is something you and your team will need to commit at least a few minutes to managing every day. This includes approving new members, driving new conversations, deleting members who violate your terms, etc. However, you can add multiple moderators/admins to your group so that responsibility doesn't all fall on you. Creating your own group for a sales or product heavy theme isn't the goal, and won't drive new members or engagement. However, having your own group allows you to create a platform for the industry topics or niche are you specialize in. And, as an owner or admin—your group members are likely to connect with you and follow your company.

As you can see, there are many ways for you to network and expand your personal profile and Company Page to a larger audience on LinkedIn. As with all organic methods of social media marketing, consistency is the key to success. You can boost all organic strategies with LinkedIn's paid advertising options.

Now as great as all of this info is, it's not going to be of any use to you or your business if you don't apply what you've learned. So, roll up your sleeves and get ready to execute the steps in the following battle plan...

Battle Plan

Step 1: Spend an hour brainstorming your LinkedIn marketing goals.

Step 2: Think about what kind of content is most useful for your business or niche and develop a content plan.

Step 3: Take 15 minutes to create and optimize a LinkedIn company page in accordance with what you learned in this guide.

Step 4: Start creating, curating, and posting the content decided on in step 2 and begin implementing the recommended practices you've learned here.

www.ingramcontent.com/pod-product-compliance
Lightning Source LLC
Chambersburg PA
CBHW071445210326
41597CB00020B/3943